Year 3

Photocopiable

Punctuation and Grammar

TOPICAL RESOURCES

Introduction

Photocopiable Punctuation and Grammar provides a variety of different activities and approaches to help Year 3 pupils understand various aspects of the English language.

It has been written with the 'Sentence Level Work' of the 'National Literacy Strategy' in mind but could be used equally as well in classes following other schemes of work.

The photocopiable pages could be used with whole classes, small groups or individual pupils at the discretion of the class teacher. They are ideal for the 'twenty minute independent activity time'.

Topical Resources
P.O. Box 329
Broughton
Preston
Lancashire
PR3 5LT

Topical Resources publishes a range of Educational Materials for use in Primary Schools and Pre-School Nurseries and Playgroups.

For latest catalogue:
Tel: 01772 863158
Fax: 01772 866153

E.mail: sales@topical-resources.co.uk
Visit our Website on:
www.topical-resources.co.uk

Copyright © 2006 Heather Bell
Illustrated and designed by Paul Sealey
Illustration & Design, 3 Wentworth Drive,
Thornton, Lancashire.

Printed in the UK for 'Topical Resources' by
T. Snape & Co. Ltd., Boltons Court, Preston,
Lancashire

First Published January 2006
ISBN-10 1 905509 01 4
ISBN-13 978 1 905509 01 0

Contents

Year 3

Term 1

Learning Objective: to recognise that sentences need capital letters and full stops.

Name: _____ Date: _____

Sentences

A **sentence** must **make sense**. It begins with a **capital letter** and often **ends with a full stop**. For example - My name is Jack.

Task 1
*Read each of these carefully and put **a ring** around the ones that are **proper sentences and which make sense**.*

1. We have two dogs.   3. Sam went to bed.   5. Come in for tea Sanjit.

2. in the garden   4. Was a tall boy   6. Emma loves ice cream.

Task 2
*Here are some beginnings and endings of sentences. **Match the correct beginning and ending**, so that they make sense. Copy each one on the lines below making sure each one begins with a capital letter and ends with a full stop. The first one has been done for you.*

SENTENCE BEGINNINGS
Little Bo Peep
The dog chased
We had lots of fire-works
Sam posted the letter
Jack and Jill

SENTENCE ENDINGS
the cat around the garden.
in the post-box.
went up the hill.
lost her sheep.
on bonfire night.

1. Little Bo Peep lost her sheep. _____

2. _____

3. _____

4. _____

5. _____

Task 3
*Finish each sentence. Don't forget the **full stop at the end**.*

1. My favourite dinner is _____

2. I like to play _____

3. My friends are _____

4. For my birthday I would like _____

5. In my bedroom there is _____

6

Name: _____   Date: _____

Sentences

A **sentence** must **make sense**. It begins with a **capital letter** and often **ends with a full stop**.
For example - This is my new toy.

Task 1   *Read these sentence endings. Now **make up a beginning** for each sentence so that it makes sense. Remember to begin each one with a capital letter.*

1._____ for our dinner.

2._____ with my pocket money.

3._____ on the farm.

4._____ for Christmas.

5._____ in town.

Task 2   *Here are some muddled sentences. Sort them out and write them on the line below. Remember to be sure **they begin with a capital letter and end with a full stop**.*

1. football to play in the garden we like

_____

2. two brothers and Muhammad one sister has

_____

3. off the trees autumn in fall the leaves

_____

4. holiday went on to Spain we

_____

5. party Jo's birthday went to Susie

_____

Task 3   *Here is some writing about Sally's pets. She has forgotten to put it in sentences.*
Mark in clearly where the capital letters and full stops should be.

sally has four pets she has two dogs called Henry and Fred sally
often takes them for walks in the park she also has a small ginger
kitten whose name is rosie rosie loves to sit on sally's knee as well
as dogs and a kitten Sally has a rabbit called Thumper

Learning Objective: to understand the need for speech marks and to know that they go around the words which are actually spoken.

Name: _____ Date: _____

Speech Marks

Speech marks are used in writing to show **the words which are spoken**. The words spoken go **inside** the speech marks. **The first word** always begins with a **capital letter** and the **punctuation mark,** at the end of the sentence, goes **inside** the speech marks. For example-
"Come to my house for tea," said Sam. "Thank-you," replied Tom.

Task 1

Write out what each person says below the picture. The first one has been done for you.

Neesha

"Knock knock, who's there?" asked Neesha.

Emma

" _____ , " replied Emma.

Neesha

" _____ ?"

asked _____ .

Emma

" _____ ?"

replied _____ .

Task 2

*Now put the **speech marks** around the words **actually spoken** in these sentences. Remember to start with a **capital letter** and don't forget the **punctuation marks**. The first one has been done for you.*

1. "Can I ride your bike?" John asked.

2. Yes, of course you can replied Luke

3. Shall we go to the park John asked

4. That's a good idea said Luke

5. I could get my bike on the way said Jo

6. We'll have great fun laughed Luke

Task 3

Now make your own cartoon of a knock knock joke. Write out what is said below the pictures using speech marks.

Learning Objective: to understand the need for speech marks and how to use them correctly.

Name: _____   Date: _____

Speech Marks

Speech marks are used in writing to show **the words which are spoken. The first word** inside the speech marks begins with a **capital letter** and the **punctuation mark,** at the end of the sentence, **goes inside the speech marks**.
For Example - "I am in the football team," said Isabella.

Task 1

*Write in what each person said. Remember to **begin** your speech with a **capital letter**.*

1. My teacher said, " _____ ."

2. The shop-keeper said, " _____ ."

3. " _____ ,"said the old lady.

4. " _____ ,"said the zoo-keeper.

Task 2

*Sometimes the speech comes at the **beginning** of the sentence. Write each sentence, putting in the speech marks.*

1. My favourite game is tennis, said Daniel.

_____

2. I love numeracy, said Lucy.

_____

3. We can swim, said the twins.

_____

4. Where are you going to on holiday? asked Dad.

_____

Task 3

*Sometimes the speech comes at the **end** of the sentence. Write each sentence putting in the speech marks.*

1. Pam said, Today is my birthday.

_____

2. Priya asked, Did you go to Town?

_____

3. Robert said, I have to be home by six.

_____

4. Mrs.Brown said, What a lovely day it is!

_____

Name: _____   Date: _____

Speech Marks

Speech marks are used in writing to show the words which are spoken. The first word inside the speech marks begins with a **capital letter** and the **punctuation mark,** at the end of the sentence, goes **inside** the speech marks.

For example - Bandu said, "We are going on holiday tomorrow."

Task 1

Write each sentence putting in the speech marks.

1. Fiona said, My gran is ill.

_____

2. Sean asked, Can I come to the party?

_____

3. You are welcome to come! the boy replied.

_____

4. The teacher shouted, Will the class please be quiet!

_____

5. The bus will leave in five minutes! shouted the driver.

_____

Task 2

*Put in the **speech marks** and **punctuation** in these sentences. The first one has been done for you.*

1. I can ride a bike said Chris

" I can ride a bike," said Chris.

2. do you like pizza asked Jim.

_____

3. we are going on cub camp said Billy and Karl

_____

4. Jon asked shall we go to the park

_____

5. the lady shouted to her dog come here Bob

_____

Task 3

*Find **two sentences** with speech in them in your reading book. Copy them carefully into your book.*

Learning Objective: to understand when question marks are needed and be able to use them.

Name: _____ Date: _____

Question Marks

Question marks are used at the **end of a question sentence**, when someone is trying to find out something. **Question sentences often begin** with the words **where, who, why, how, when**, and **what**. For example - Where are you going**?**

Task 1

Write out these question sentences beginning each one with a capital letter and ending with a question mark. The first one has been done for you.

1. how are you feeling   How are you feeling? _____

2. when is it your birthday   _____

3. why is Sam crying   _____

4. where are my slippers   _____

5. who are you sitting with   _____

6. what is the time   _____

Task 2

Here are some answers to some questions. Write the question, which you think, was asked. The first one has been done for you.

1. I go to bed at nine o'clock.   What time do you go to bed? _____

2. On Saturday I go to town.   _____

3. I am laughing at a very funny joke. _____

4. My best friend is called Jo.   _____

5. Use crayons to colour with.   _____

6. Ten add ten makes twenty.   _____

Task 3

*Look at your reading book. Find **two question** sentences and copy them into your book.*

11

Name: _____ Date: _____

Question Marks

Question marks are used at the **end of a question sentence**, when someone is trying to find out something. For example - Can I play with you? **Question sentences sometimes begin** with the words **where, who, why, how, what** and **when**. For example - Where are you going?

Task 1

Look at the picture below of a busy road. Make up eight question sentences about it and get a friend to answer them.

1. _____

2. _____

3. _____

4. _____

5. _____

6. _____

7. _____

8. _____

Task 2

*Look in your reading book and find **two** question sentences, which do not begin with where, who, what, why, how or when. Copy them into your book.*

Learning Objective: to understand when exclamation marks are needed and to be able to use them.

Name: _____   Date: _____

Exclamation Marks

Exclamation sentences tell us that something exciting has happened or that someone feels very strongly about the event. Exclamation sentences begin with a **capital letter** and end with an **exclamation mark**.
For example - What a wonderful day it was! Be quiet class five!

Task 1

Write each of these exclamation sentences correctly, putting in the capital letter at the start and the exclamation mark at the end.

1. don't be so nasty

_____

2. the play was fantastic

_____

3. stop shouting out

_____

4. be careful crossing the road

_____

5. i love pizza

_____

6. what a beautiful picture

_____

Task 2

Only some of these sentences are exclamation sentences. Use a coloured pencil and put either a full stop or an exclamation mark at the end of the sentence.

1. I hate sprouts

3. Today is Tuesday

5. She goes on the bus

2. Go to bed now

4. What an amazing sunset

6. She adores ice-cream

Task 3

Write each sentence correctly. There are three question sentences and three exclamation sentences.

1. what a clever boy

_____

2. who can play today

_____

3. he loves chocolate

_____

4. do you go to Cubs

_____

5. can you swim

_____

6. sam is such a good baby

_____

Learning Objective: to understand when exclamation marks are needed and to be able to use them.

Name: _____   Date: _____

Exclamation Marks

Exclamation sentences tell us that something **exciting** has happened or that someone feels very **strongly** about the event. **Exclamation sentences** begin with a **capital letter** and end with an **exclamation mark**. They often begin with the words **what** or **how**. For example - How cold it is! What a stupid boy!

Task 1   *Make these sentences into exclamation sentences using the word **what** to open each one. The first one has been done for you.*

1. He is a tall man.   What a tall man he is! _____

2. It is a good dog.   _____

3. It is a calm sea.   _____

4. It is a beautiful day. _____

5. It is a strong wind.   _____

6. It is heavy rain.   _____

Task 2   *Read the passage. It has no sentences . Put it into **SEVEN sentences**. There are **TWO exclamation** sentences and **TWO question** sentences. Write it out correctly below.*

it was Emma's birthday she was so excited what presents might she be given she ran downstairs Emma felt really happy where might the presents be they were piled up on the kitchen table

_____

_____

_____

_____

_____

_____

Task 3
*Find **two exclamation sentences** in your reading book. Write them into your book.*

Name: _____ Date: _____

Commas in Lists

Commas are used in **lists** to mark off **separate items**. A comma is **not** needed before the word 'and'. For example – **The greedy boy ate six cream cakes, two packets of crisps, four packets of sweets and a bar of chocolate.**

Task 1

Copy these sentences on the line below, putting in the missing commas.

1. At the zoo we saw two snakes four seals three penguins and an elephant.

   _____

2. For Christmas I was given a book two pens a model car and a TV.

   _____

3. On a school visit we need lunch strong shoes a note-pad and a coat.

   _____

4. The monster had three eyes two heads a slimy body and a tail.

   _____

5. My uncle has visited Spain France Africa India and America.

   _____

6. We painted pictures of Sanjit Anna Jim Priya and Harry in art.

   _____

Task 2

Make up sentences with commas in lists using these words.

1. tea – fish chips peas salt vinegar

   _____

2. garden – roses tulips daffodils

   _____

3. pet shop – hamsters rabbits snakes spiders

   _____

4. band – guitar drums piano trumpet flute

   _____

5. weather – sunny windy snowy wet

   _____

6. cake – butter sugar flour eggs

   _____

Task 3

*Look through your reading book - can you find a **sentence** with **commas in a list**? Copy it into your book.*

Name:_____   Date:_____

Commas in Lists

Commas are used in lists to mark off **separate items**. A comma is not needed before the word 'and'. For example - The boy had a rat, a fish, two cats and a dog

Task 1

Find the correct ending for each sentence. Copy it out on the lines below – don't forget the commas!

1. Some capital cities are	Chelsea Everton and Arsenal.
2. To grow seeds you need	Paris London and Rome.
3. Some insects are	carrots onions beans and leeks.
4. Three English cities are	a plant pot soil and water.
5. The man grew	London Leeds and Birmingham.
6. Some football teams are	ants beetles and ladybirds.

1._____

2._____

3._____

4._____

5._____

6._____

Task 2

Commas are often used to separate instructions. *Number these instructions in the right order, one to six. Write your numbers in the small boxes.*

remove the tea bag,	and enjoy your tea!	Put water into the kettle to boil,
add milk and sugar	pour boiling water into the cup,	put a tea bag into the cup,

Task 3

Write instructions in a list with commas to make a slice of toast.

Learning Objective: to understand the use of verbs and be able to use these in sentences.

Name: _____ Date: _____

Verbs

All **sentences** must have a **verb** if they are to make sense. Verbs tell us what someone is doing. For example – The boy **played** football.

Task 1 *Put **a ring** around the **verbs** in these sentences.*

1. The frog hopped into the pond.

2. The dog chased the cat.

3. The girl is singing a song.

4. We are walking home.

5. The sun is shining in the sky.

6. The bird flew into the tree.

Task 2 *Choose the **correct verb** to make each of these sentences make sense.*

1. The artist_____ a picture.

2. The gardener _____ the lawns.

3. The little fish_____ in the stream.

4. The footballer_____ the ball in the net.

5. The horse _____ across the field.

6. The rain _____ on the window pane.

7. The dog _____ the bone.

8. The window-cleaner_____ the windows.

mowed
chewed
galloped
swam
washed
kicked
splashed
painted

Task 3 *Put **a ring** around the **verbs** in this passage.*

Sam heard a noise. He climbed out of bed and looked round the room. He saw no one. Then he heard it again. Sam opened the door. He walked on to the landing. Suddenly he saw the problem. Rosie the cat had knocked over a plant pot!

Learning Objective: to understand the use of verbs and be able to use these in sentences.

Name: _____ Date: _____

Verbs

All **sentences** must have a **verb** if they are to make sense. Verbs tell us what someone is doing. For example – The boy **played** football.

Task 1   *Put **a ring** around the **verbs** in these sentences. Then copy the sentence and change the verb for another that has the same meaning from the box. The first one has been done for you.*

laughed	cried	
~~spoke~~	fried	began
changed	finished	picked

1. Tom (talked) to his friend Dan.   Tom spoke to his friend Dan. _____

2. Ben giggled at the joke. _____

3. We chose a chocolate. _____

4. They started the test. _____

5. The boy howled when he fell. _____

6. The green leaves turned to yellow. _____

7. The play ended at nine o'clock. _____

8. The fish sizzled in the pan. _____

Task 2   *Link verbs which mean the **opposite** from the boxes below. Write the pairs on the lines. The first one has been done for you.*

close	whisper
stand	push
shout	leave
die	sit
pull	take
give	cry
forget	live
spend	remember
laugh	open
arrive	save

1. close / open _____   6. _____

2. _____   7. _____

3. _____   8. _____

4. _____   9. _____

5. _____   10. _____

Task 3   *Now look at your reading book. **Find 10 verbs**. Copy them into your book.*

18   © Topical Resources. May be photocopied for classroom use only.

Learning Objective: to collect verbs which are related in meaning and to understand that choosing interesting verbs can improve sentences.

Name: _____ Date: _____

Verbs

All **sentences** must have a **verb** if they are to make sense. Choosing interesting verbs can improve sentences.
For example – 'The sun **shone** in the sky' could be changed to 'The sun **blazed** in the sky'. Blazed tells us that the day was very hot. It makes the sentence more exciting.

Task 1   *Take each of these sentences and write them on the line **changing the verb to a more interesting one** from the box below. The first one has been done for you.*

| buzzed | crept | lashed | leapt | gushed | pounced | ~~howled~~ |

1. The wind <u>blew</u> through the trees.   The wind howled through the trees.

2. The rain <u>hit</u> against the window.   _____

3. The bee <u>flew</u> in the classroom.   _____

4. The boy <u>jumped</u> on his friend.   _____

5. The burglar <u>walked</u> round the house.   _____

6. The cat <u>jumped</u> on the mouse.   _____

7. The water <u>came</u> out of the tap.   _____

Task 2   *Read the paragraph carefully. The **verbs** have been **underlined** for you. Copy it, **replacing the verbs** with **more exciting** ones.*

Joseph <u>went</u> into the empty house. He <u>looked</u> around him. He <u>said</u>, "Is there anyone there?" He <u>said</u> it in a quiet, frightened voice. He <u>went</u> up the stairs and looked around him. Joe <u>put</u> <u>out</u> his hands. Something furry <u>went</u> past his legs and Joe <u>went</u> back out of the house as fast as he could. He <u>screamed</u> in fear.

_____

_____

_____

_____

_____

_____

Task 3

*Now look through your reading book and find **6 exciting verbs**. Copy them into your book.*

19

Name: _____   Date: _____

Verbs – Past Tense of Regular Verbs

We talk about **verbs** being in the present tense when they tell us **what is happening now**. For example – **I am walking my dog**. When we talk about **what happened yesterday**, the verb is written in the **past tense** – Yesterday I **walked** my dog. When we make regular verbs into the **past tense**, we add 'ed'. For example – **walk** becomes **walked**.

Task 1   *In these sentences the verbs are written in the present tense. Write them in the **past tense** as though they happened yesterday. The first one has been done for you.*

1. I <u>am playing</u> the piano.   Yesterday I played the piano. _____

2. Billy <u>is painting</u> a picture.   Yesterday _____

3. They <u>are watching</u> T.V.   Yesterday _____

4. He <u>is baking</u> a loaf of bread.   Yesterday _____

5. Bandu <u>is climbing</u> over the wall. Yesterday _____

6. I <u>am moving</u> house.   Yesterday _____

7. She <u>is opening</u> a box of sweets.   Yesterday _____

Task 2   *This time change the verbs **from the past to the present tense**. The first one has been done for you.*

1. Yesterday I <u>walked</u> to school.   Today I am walking to school. _____

2. Yesterday mum <u>was ill</u>.   Today _____

3. Yesterday we <u>ran</u> home.   Today _____

4. Yesterday he <u>cooked</u> the dinner.   Today _____

5. Yesterday the boy <u>worked</u> hard.   Today _____

6. Yesterday the old lady <u>was tired</u>.   Today _____

7. Yesterday they <u>brushed</u> the horse.   Today _____

Task 3   *Now find 5 examples of verbs in the past tense from your reading book.*

Learning Objective: to be able to understand and use the past tense of irregular verbs.

Name: _____   Date: _____

Verbs – Past Tense of Irregular Verbs

When we put **regular verbs** into the **past tense**, we add 'ed'. For example – 'I **walk** the dog' (present) becomes 'I **walked** the dog' (past). **Some verbs are 'irregular'**. When we change them from the present tense to the past tense we cannot just add 'ed'. For example – 'I **am writing** a story' becomes 'I **wrote** a story' when changed into the past tense.

Task 1

*Choose the verb from the **present tense box** and the verb from the **past tense box**, which **go together** and write them on the line.*

present tense verbs	past tense verbs
know	drew
draw	won
run	saw
win	found
find	wrote
see	knew
blow	blew
write	ran

1. know   /   knew
2. _____ / _____
3. _____ / _____
4. _____ / _____
5. _____ / _____
6. _____ / _____
7. _____ / _____
8. _____ / _____

Task 2

*The paragraph below is written in the present tense. Write it in the **past tense**.* The verbs which need to be changed are underlined to help you.

I **am going** to visit my Grandma. I **am taking** the path through the woods. Suddenly I **see** lots of flowers. They **are growing** under the trees. A wolf **is coming** down the path. I **am running** away. He **knows** I **am** frightened.

_____

_____

_____

_____

_____

Task 3

*Now find **6 irregular verbs in the past tense** in your reading book.*

Name: _____ Date: _____

Verbs – Past Tense of Irregular Verbs

Task 1

The past tenses of these verbs have been written wrongly. Write them out correctly, choosing the correct irregular past tense verb from the box below.

felt	sang	brought	fell
flew	found	wore	knew

1. He knowed his spellings. _____

2. I feeled very ill. _____

3. She brunged her dog. _____

4. The canary flyed away. _____

5. The boy sunged a solo. _____

6. He finded a pound coin. _____

7. The baby falled asleep. _____

8. She weared a new hat. _____

Task 2   *Ring the irregular and past tense verbs in the paragraph below. These are incorrect. Write what they should be above them.*

Fiona waked up. It were a lovely day. The sun shined in the sky. The birds

sanged in the trees. She feeled happy! Then she runned downstairs and eated

her breakfast quickly. Fiona goed in the garden, where she seed her Mum.

Her Mum were looking at all the flowers that growed there.

MAGIC MOON BOOTS

What can these *amazing boots* do?
Walk *up walls, across ceilings* and
help you to hang *upside down*!

From Jones' Toy Shop
St John's Street
Open Monday to Saturday
9.00am – 6.00pm

**Bargain
Price
£19.99**

Only 20 pairs at special offer price. Rest sold at full price of £99

Name: _____   Date: _____

Different Ways of Presenting Text

Words are printed in different ways to make them more effective. Sometimes **bold print** is used; sometimes whole words are written in **capital letters** or even **very small letters**. Sometimes words are in *italics* or are underlined, so that we notice them.

Task 1   *Look at the leaflet for Moon Boots.*

1. Write two words written in bold text?

_____

2. Write three words in italicised type?

_____

3. Why do you think the title MAGIC MOON BOOTS is in capital letters?

_____

4. Why is the information at the bottom of the advert in very small print?

_____

5. Why is "Bargain Price" written inside a star in large lettering?

Task 2   *Now design an advert of your own for a MAGIC **CARPET** – don't forget to put **the price**, **where and when** you can buy it and what its **special features** are.*

Name: _____   Date: _____

Punctuation of Sentences

A **sentence** must **make sense**. It begins with a **capital letter** and often **ends with a full stop**. For example – My name is Ben.

Task 1

*Put **a tick** next to each of these **only if it is a proper sentence** that makes **sense** and has a **capital letter** and **full stop**.*

1. My cat is called Holly. ☐   5. Tom ate a sweet. ☐

2. Gina plays the piano. ☐   6. In the rain. ☐

3. My teacher is kind. ☐   7. went on holiday. ☐

4. our house is near school. ☐   8. We give them a present. ☐

*Now make the ones which were **not proper sentences into correctly punctuated ones**. You may need to add more words so that they make sense. Write them on the lines below.*

1. _____

2. _____

3. _____

Task 2

*Here is a short paragraph about Dan's visit to the zoo. Mark in the **capital letters** and **full stops**. Then write **4 more sentences** that Dan might have written on the lines below.*

Some words to help you – seals	penguins	snakes	zoo-keeper
reptiles monkeys	dinner	giraffes	tigers

Dan went with his mum to the zoo the zoo was in Blackpool they got there early in

the morning Dan and his mum went to see the lions next they saw three elephants

at twelve o'clock there was a parrot show they did lots of tricks

_____

_____

_____

_____

Name: _____ Date: _____

Punctuation of Sentences

A sentence must **make sense**. It begins with a **capital letter** and ends with a **full stop**.
For example – My name is Ben.

Task 1 These sentences make a short story. **Number them in order from 1 to 6 so that the story makes sense**. Then copy them out in the correct order remembering to make sure they have **capital letters** and **full stops**.

☐ First I have a wash and brush my teeth.
☐ Then I get dressed.
☐ At half past eight I walk to school.
☐ I get to school by nine o'clock.
☐ I get out of bed at eight o'clock.
☐ Next I eat my breakfast.

1. _____

2. _____

3. _____

4. _____

5. _____

6. _____

Task 2 Now write **six sentences** explaining what you do before you go to bed.

1. _____

2. _____

3. _____

4. _____

5. _____

6. _____

Date: _____

Commas in Lists

Commas are used in **lists** to mark off **separate items**. A comma is **not needed before the word 'and'**. For example – The greedy boy ate six cream cakes, two packets of crisps, four packets of sweets and a bar of chocolate.

Task 1   *Write these sentences out correctly on the line below remembering to use commas.*

1. The gardener grew apples pears onions and potatoes.

_____

2. The boy could play the piano a trumpet and a guitar.

_____

3. For the party we made jelly cakes sandwiches and salad.

_____

4. I packed a t-shirt socks jeans and a toothbrush.

_____

5. At school we had a spellings tables and a history test.

_____

Task 2   *Now make up sentences with lists about -*

1. family

_____

2. favourite food

_____

3. films

_____

4. zoo animals

_____

5. farm animals

_____

Task 3   *Can you find an example of a sentence with commas in a list in your reading book? Copy it into your book.*

27

Year 3
Term 2

Name:_____   Date:_____

Common Nouns

Nouns are names of objects. For example – table, chair and car are nouns.
A noun is a word which names **a place**, **an object**, **a person or an animal**.

Task 1   *Look at this seaside picture. List **eight nouns** from the picture. The first one has been done for you.*

1. deckchair_____

2. _____

3. _____

4. _____

5. _____

6. _____

7. _____

8. _____

Task 2

*Now using the words in the box below choose the correct **noun** to complete each sentence.*

cup	rabbit	legs	baker	films	eggs	apple	spade	cow	doctor

1. An _____ is a type of fruit.

2. A _____ bakes bread.

3. We drink tea from a _____.

4. A _____ has long ears.

5. You watch _____ at the cinema.

6. Bob digs the garden with a _____.

7. A spider has eight_____.

8. A _____ makes people better.

9. A hen lays _____.

10. Milk comes from a _____.

Task 3   *Finally, make up five sentences of your own using these common nouns.*

1. children, school _____

2. park, swing _____

3. party, cakes _____

4. pond, ducks _____

5. circus, clown _____

Learning Objective: to understand and use common nouns.

Name: _____ Date: _____

Common Nouns

Nouns are names of objects. For example – table, chair and car are nouns.
A noun is a word which names **a place**, **an object**, **a person or an animal**.

Task 1 *Read this carefully. Make a list of the ten common nouns on the lines below.*

We went to the fair. I had a ride on the big wheel, the dodgems and the boats. My Mum bought me a candy floss. I won a teddy and a balloon. My friend went on a swing. Later we had chips.

1. _____ 2. _____ 3. _____ 4. _____ 5. _____

6. _____ 7. _____ 8. _____ 9. _____ 10. _____

Task 2 *Complete each of the sentences by choosing* **a common noun** *from the box below.*

game	flower	jewel	fruit	shop
fish	animal	building	tree	meat

1. Football is a _____ .

2. A ruby is a _____ .

3. A daffodil is a _____ .

4. A zebra is an _____ .

5. A banana is a _____ .

6. Pork is a kind of _____ .

7. A supermarket is a kind of _____ .

8. A castle is a kind of _____ .

9. Cod is a kind of _____ .

10. An oak is a kind of _____ .

Task 3 *Fill in each box with as many common nouns as you can think of.*

Vegetables	Jobs	Transport

Learning Objective: to understand the term proper nouns and be able to use them.

Name: _____   Date: _____

Proper Nouns

A **proper noun** is a **special name** for a **person or thing**. For example – Jim (names),
Glasgow (cities), Spain (countries), June (months), the Thames (rivers),
Venus (planets) and Monday (days). **These all begin with a capital letter.**

Task 1   *Put **capital letters** in the following sentences.*

1. ben is my best friend.

_____

2. saturn is a planet.

_____

3. leeds is a city.

_____

4. france is a country.

_____

5. february is the shortest month.

_____

6. the avon is a river.

_____

7. saturday is at the weekend.

_____

8. I know a girl called kate.

_____

9. the alps are mountains.

_____

10. the ship was called the titanic.

_____

Task 2   *Here are some **common nouns**. For each one find a **proper noun**. The first one has been done for you.*

1. river -   Lune _____

2. ocean -   _____

3. month -   _____

4. boy -   _____

5. girl -   _____

6. planet -   _____

7. country -   _____

8. town -   _____

9. mountain -   _____

10. island -   _____

Task 3   *Look at your reading book. Find **5 different proper nouns**. Write them in your book.*

Learning Objective: to understand the term proper nouns and be able to use them.

Name: _____   Date: _____

Proper Nouns

A **proper noun** is a **special name** for a **person or thing**. For example –
Jim (names), Glasgow (cities), Spain (countries), June (months), the Thames (rivers),
Venus (planets) and Monday (days). **These all begin with a capital letter**.

Task 1   *Copy these sentences and put in the **capital letters** at the
beginning of each proper noun.*

1. jack and jill went up the hill.

_____

2. on tuesday we went to london.

_____

3. the sahara desert is in africa.

_____

4. alexander graham bell invented the telephone.

_____

5. everest is the highest mountain.

_____

6. loch ness is in scotland.

_____

7. arsenal is a famous football team.

_____

8. the times is a newspaper.

_____

Task 2   ***Unjumble** these **names**.*

1. amS _____   4. treRbo _____

2. mmEa _____   5. hoJn _____

3. amGem _____   6. cJak _____

Task 3   ***Unjumble** these **days of the week**.*

1. yaMdon _____   3. nuSady _____

2. deWsenyad _____   4. hurTsyad _____

Task 4   ***Unjumble** these **months**.*

1. charM _____   3. nuJe _____

2. yaM _____   4. lyuJ _____

Learning Objective: to understand the term collective nouns and be able to use them.

Name: _____ Date: _____

Collective Nouns

Collective nouns describe **a group of things**. They **do not need** to begin with a **capital letter**.
For example – a bunch of flowers, a herd of cows.

Task 1

Choose a **collective noun** from the box below to complete these phrases.

choir	team	army	crowd	shoal	galaxy
forest	pack	litter	bunch	library	class

1. a _____ of grapes

2. a _____ of singers

3. an _____ of soldiers

4. a _____ of people

5. a _____ of cricketers

6. a _____ of fish

7. a _____ of trees

8. a _____ of stars

9. a _____ of cards

10. a _____ of books

11. a _____ of children

12. a _____ of puppies

Task 2

Match the correct **collective noun** with its **group**.

1. a bundle of   monkeys

2. a shoal of   wolves

3. a pride of   whales

4. a school of   bees

5. a gang of   fish

6. a pack of   sticks

7. a swarm of   lions

8. a troop of   thieves

Task 3

Here are some **tricky collective nouns** to look up in your dictionary.
Write down their meaning.

a. orchestra   _____

b. constellation   _____

c. troupe   _____

Learning Objective: to understand the term collective nouns and be able to use them.

Name: _____   Date: _____

Collective Nouns

A **collective noun** is a **name** which tells us about a **group** of things.
For example – A flock of sheep or a library of books.

Task 1

*Look at the Word Search below. There are **8 collective nouns**.
Can you find them?*

b	a	p	a	c	k	e	t
j	y	f	l	o	c	k	e
s	h	o	a	l	f	w	a
r	a	o	z	l	o	b	m
i	g	u	h	e	r	d	s
n	a	l	x	c	e	t	a
n	n	i	b	t	s	m	n
s	g	p	o	i	t	c	f
e	a	r	o	o	s	q	t
l	t	o	t	n	r	p	r

packet

collection

shoal

herd

team

gang

flock

forest

Task 2

Now make up sentences for six of them. The first one has been done for you.

1. I ate a packet of chocolate biscuits. _____

2. _____

3. _____

4. _____

5. _____

6. _____

Task 3

Invent some collective nouns of your own for each of these.

puppies -   A pen of a playful poodle puppies. _____

smugglers - _____

magicians - _____

aliens - _____

skate-boards - _____

Name: _____   Date: _____

Singular and Plural

Nouns are **singular** if there is **only one** of them, or **plural** if there are more than one.
For example – One dog but two dog**s**

Task 1   *Complete this list putting in the **singular or plural**.*

Singular		Plural
one boy	⟶	two _____
one key	⟶	two _____
one_____	⟶	two giraffes
one_____	⟶	two men
one story	⟶	two _____
one _____	⟶	two wolves
one_____	⟶	two ladies
one child	⟶	two _____
one tooth	⟶	two _____
one _____	⟶	two hats

Task 2   *Change these sentences from **singular into plural**. The first one is done for you.*

1. The boy plays with his toy.   The boys play with their toys. _____

2. The girl sings a song.   _____

3. Our car needs a new tyre.   _____

4. My cousin has a dog.   _____

5. The bird sings in the tree.   _____

6. The hen lays an egg.   _____

Task 3   *Now look in your reading book, find **5 singular nouns** and **5 plural nouns**.*

Learning Objective: to understand the idea of singular and plural and to be able to use these correctly.

Name: _____   Date: _____

Singular and Plural

Nouns are **singular** if there is **only one** of them, or **plural** if there are more than one. For example – One dog but two dogs.

Task 1

*Change these sentences from **plural into singular**. The first one has been done for you.*

1. The houses have two doors.   The house has one door.

2. The cats have three kittens.   _____

3. My uncles have two cars.   _____

4. The boys play in the parks.   _____

5. The mice eat some sweets.   _____

6. The flowers have two leaves.   _____

Task 2

Some words can be both singular and plural. *For example – deer. Here are some pictures and some muddled words. Sort them out.*

ered

_____

peshe

_____

restrous

_____

roshts

_____

ssiscors

_____

roufl

_____

Task 3

*Here are some words which have **unusual plurals**. Write them on the lines below.*

man _____   child _____

woman _____   goose _____

foot _____   mouse _____

Learning Objective: to understand that capital letters are used sometimes to create special emphasis and for headings.

Name: _____   Date: _____

Other Uses of Capital Letters in Text

Words are sometimes written in **capital letters** when they are **part of a heading**.
For example – BANK RAID ON LOCAL SHOP! **Capital letters** can also be
used to create **special emphasis in a sentence**.
For example – The dog was ENORMOUS!

Task 1   *Make up some newspaper headings for each of these
stories. Make each one seem exciting and write it in capital letters.*

1. A lion breaks loose from the   LION BREAKS LOOSE FROM SAFARI PARK!
   local Safari Park.

2. A famous pop star visits
   your area.

3. A grandma swims across
   the Channel to France.

4. A local school has a visit
   from the Queen.

5. A strange animal is spotted
   on the local moor.

6. Heavy rain causes a flood
   at the local school.

7. A local boy is chosen to
   be in a TV play.

Task 2   *Sometimes just **one word** in a sentence **is put in capital letters** to make **the idea
stand out** as very important. Decide which word needs to have capital letters and write the sentence
on the line. The first one has been done for you.*

1. The child cried so loudly it woke us up.   The child cried so LOUDLY it woke us up.

2. Who's been eating my porridge?

3. The naughty boy screamed.

4. The tree was very tall.

5. "Be quiet!" shouted the teacher.

6. "I am important," said the Queen.

7. "Stand still," ordered the soldier.

© Topical Resources. May be photocopied for classroom use only.

Name: _____ Date: _____

Other Uses of Capital Letters in Text - Poetry

Sometimes the **first word** on a **new line** of a **poem** begins with a **capital letter**.

Task 1

*Read this poem carefully. Notice how each line **begins** with a **capital letter**.*

SUNDAY!

Sunday
Late mornings, cuddled up in my duvet by the fire.
Sunday
The peal of church bells in the distance.
Sunday
Dads chattering as they wash the car.
Sunday
The wafting smell of roast dinners.
Sunday
Walks with my dog in the park.
Sunday
Waiting for Monday and another week of school.

Task 2

Now write a poem about Monday in the space below. Remember to set it out like the Sunday poem and begin each line with a capital letter.

MONDAY!

_____

_____

_____

_____

_____

_____

_____

_____

_____

_____

_____

Learning Objective: to understand the function of adjectives within sentences and to be able to use them in writing.

Name: _____   Date: _____

Adjectives

An **adjective** tells us **more** about a **noun**. It is a **describing word**.
For example – the **red** car, the **old** lady

Task 1   *Underline the **adjectives** in the phrases below.*

1. the black dog

2. the new toy

3. the tiny mouse

4. the ugly monster

5. the sunny day

6. the silver necklace

7. the juicy apple

8. the pretty flower

9. the long story

10. the empty street

Task 2   *Now think of an **adjective** to complete these phrases.* **Do not use the same one twice.**

1. the _____princess

2. the _____cat

3. the _____teacher

4. the _____car

5. the _____road

6. the _____dinner

7. the_____day

8. the _____child

9. the _____picture

10. the _____lady

Task 3   *Now look through your reading book, find **eight phrases** which have an **adjective** in them. Copy them here.*

1. _____

2. _____

3. _____

4. _____

5. _____

6. _____

7. _____

8. _____

Learning Objective: to understand the function of adjectives within sentences and to be able to use them in writing.

Name: _____   Date: _____

Adjectives

An **adjective** tells us **more** about a **noun**. **It is a describing word**.
For example – the **red** car, the **old** lady

Task 1
People often use the **adjective 'nice'** when they could use a much better and more descriptive word. **Change the word 'nice' for a better adjective. Do not use any adjective more than once.** Write the sentence on the line below.

1. a <u>nice</u> bunch of grapes
   a juicy bunch of grapes

2. a <u>nice</u> breakfast
   _____

3. a <u>nice</u> tune
   _____

4. a <u>nice</u> garden
   _____

5. a <u>nice</u> smell
   _____

6. a <u>nice</u> present
   _____

7. a <u>nice</u> sweet
   _____

8. a <u>nice</u> house
   _____

9. a <u>nice</u> holiday
   _____

10. a <u>nice</u> bike
    _____

Task 2
Change the **adjectives** in these sentences so that the sentence is interesting and still makes sense. The first one has been done for you.

1. The dress is green.   The dress is frilly. _____

2. My house is big.   _____

3. His book was long.   _____

4. The dog was large.   _____

5. The garden was tidy.   _____

6. The meal was huge.   _____

7. The ring was shiny.   _____

8. The lesson was interesting. _____

Task 3   Collect **6 more adjectives** in each box

Size big little	**Colour** bright red	**Taste** delicious sweet

Learning Objective: to understand the function of adjectives within sentences and to be able to use them in writing.

Name: _____   Date: _____

Adjectives

An **adjective** tells us **more** about a **noun**. **It is a describing word.**
For example – the **red** car, the **old** lady

Task 1   *Change the **adjective** in the following phrases, to one that means the **opposite**. The first one has been done for you.*

1. the happy boy   the sad boy_____   6. the careless child_____

2. the dark room   _____   7. the wealthy prince_____

3. the wealthy lady   _____   8. the modern car   _____

4. the dirty shoes   _____   9. the shiny badge   _____

5. the loud music   _____   10. the brave soldier _____

Task 2   *Sometimes we **exaggerate** when we describe things. **Change the adjectives** in these sentences so that they sound **more truthful**. The first one has been done for you.*

1. The boy was gigantic.   The boy was tall._____

2. The man was furious.   _____

3. The lady was beautiful.   _____

4. The day was freezing.   _____

5. The weather was glorious. _____

6. The child was brilliant.   _____

7. The dress was stunning.   _____

8. The toothache was agonizing. _____

9. The elephant was massive. _____

10. The light was dazzling.   _____

Task 3

*Look at the picture of the witch. **Find as many adjectives to describe her** as you can. Write them in your book.*

Name: _____   Date: _____

Essential Words in Sentences

Some words are essential in sentences if they are to make sense. A sentence must have a verb. For example – The man broke his arm. Sometimes words are added into sentences which are **not essential to their meaning.** For example – The **old**, **tired** man, **who lives in Green Street**, broke his arm. This could be simply written – The man broke his arm.

Task 1   *Read each of the sentences below. **Cross out the words which are not important** then write out the simple sentence. The first one has been done for you.*

1. The ~~beautiful~~ princess wore a ~~golden~~ dress.

   The princess wore a dress. _____

2. The tall boy was a wonderful footballer.

   _____

3. The small tabby cat chased the brown mouse.

   _____

4. My oldest and favourite sister is a talented dancer.

   _____

5. The ugly, evil witch cast a terrible spell.

   _____

6. The man-eating monster ate the small, blonde boy.

   _____

7. The grey-haired old man fell off his new blue bike.

   _____

Task 2   *This time add at least **two descriptive words** to these sentences to make them more exciting. The first one has been done for you.*

1. The boy drew a picture.

   The clever boy drew an interesting picture. _____

2. The girl sang a song.

   _____

3. The dress was worn by the princess.

   _____

4. The chest was filled with jewels.

   _____

5. The teacher shouted at the boy.

   _____

Task 3   *Now look at your reading book and **find a descriptive sentence**. Copy it in your book.*

Name: _____   Date: _____

Personal Pronouns

A **personal pronoun** stands **in place of a noun**. For example – Emma was sad
so **she** cried. **Other personal pronouns are I, me, he, we, us, you, they, it, them.**

Task 1   *Choose the **personal pronouns** that you need from the box to make each
sentence make sense. The first one has been done for you.*

1. Tom was tired so <u>he</u> went to bed.

2. Sam said to Tom, "_____ could do our homework together."

3. The house was dark and _____ was empty too.

4. I asked my friend, "Have _____ got any money?"

5. I ate some strawberries and _____ were delicious.

6. We shouted to Priya and Jon, "Come with _____ to the football match.

7. My Aunt and Uncle asked us to go with _____ on holiday.

8. _____ is a very pretty girl.

9. _____ like sprouts but my brother does not.

10. "Will you come with _____ to the shop?" I asked Sally.

he
me
them
they
it
we
I
she
us
you

Task 2   *Put a **ring around the pronouns** in the writing below.*

We have lots of pets. I have a hamster. It is called Sparky. My sister has two

cats. They are brother and sister. You can tell they are by their colour and

markings. My Dad has a dog which he calls Spot. We take him to the park.

Mum has a snake which she loves dearly.

Task 3   *Now look at your reading book. **Find two sentences with pronouns in them.**
Copy them both here and **underline the pronouns**.*

1 _____

_____

_____

2 _____

_____

Learning Objective: to understand the difference between first person pronoun singular and first person pronoun plural.

Name: _____   Date: _____

1st Person Pronouns

A **personal pronoun** stands **in place** of a **noun**. When we write about ourselves we use the word **'I'** **1st person singular** or **'we'** **1st person plural**.

Task 1

Change each of these sentences from 1st person singular to 1st person plural. The first one has been done for you.

1. I love my Grandma.   We love our Grandma. _____

2. I play with my football. _____

3. I have a dog. _____

4. I did my homework. _____

5. I go to my Aunt's house. _____

6. I go on holiday. _____

Task 2

Now change these sentences from 'we' to 'I'. The first one has been done for you.

1. We go into our tent.   I go into my tent. _____

2. We have our tea. _____

3. We play in our garden. _____

4. We got our sums correct. _____

5. We went to the zoo. _____

6. We play on our bikes. _____

Task 3

Write 2 sentences that begin with 'I like' and 2 sentences that begin 'We like'

1. _____

2. _____

3. _____

4. _____

Name: _____   Date: _____

2nd and 3rd Person Pronouns

A personal pronoun stands in place of a noun. When we talk or write to other people, we use the 2nd person pronouns, 'you'.
For example – **You** can come to play. **When we write or talk about other people we use 3rd person pronouns like he, she, it or they.**

Task 1   *We often use **2nd person pronouns** when we are writing instructions. Complete this by using the **2nd person pronouns** from the box below.*

your	yourself	your	you	yourself	you	you
yourself	you					

When _____ make a cup of tea by _____, make sure _____

mum or dad knows _____ are doing it. It is easy to burn _____.

_____ dad will show _____ how to do it. Then _____ will be

pleased with _____.

Task 2   *This writing is written in the 3rd person. **Underline all the third person pronouns**.*

Billy was a boy who liked riding his bike. One day he set off for a long ride.

After a mile, he noticed his tyre was flat. He got off his bike and wondered

what he could do. Suddenly his dad drove past in his car. He stopped.

Task 3   *Finish off the story telling how Billy's dad helped him. **Remember to continue writing in the 3rd person**.*

_____

_____

_____

_____

_____

_____

_____

_____

Learning Objective: to understand the need for agreement in sentences.

Name: _____   Date: _____

Agreement in Sentences

All **sentences** have a **verb** and this has a **subject**.
For example – **I** go (**'I' is the subject of the verb 'to go'**.) **The subject and verb must agree**. It would be wrong to say 'I goes'.

Task 1   *In these sentences the **wrong verb** has been used. **Write out the correct sentence**. The first one has been done for you.*

1. We goes to school.   We go to school.

2. The boy were tall.   _____

3. It were a lovely day.   _____

4. They was going on holiday. _____

5. She were sick.   _____

6. I goes to the shop.   _____

7. He were stood outside.   _____

Task 2   *Change these sentences **from the singular into the plural. Make sure the subject and verbs agree**. The first one has been done for you.*

1. I go to bed.   We go to bed.

2. The cat climbs the tree.   _____

3. The van travels quickly.   _____

4. The boy plays the piano.   _____

5. The clock ticks loudly.   _____

6. I have a holiday.   _____

7. The teacher has a holiday.   _____

8. The man goes to town.   _____

Task 3   *Now choose a **singular sentence** from your reading book. Copy it here, and then write it below in the plural.*

_____

_____

Name: _____   Date: _____

Agreement in Sentences

All **sentences** have a **verb**. The **verb** always has a **subject**.
For example – **I** go. (**'I' is the subject of the verb 'go'**.)
The subject and verb must agree. It would be wrong to say 'I goes'.

Task 1   *Highlight the verbs which are wrong in this story, then write it out correctly on the lines below. Remember it is all in the past tense.*

One day we was in the park. We come to the pond and see that a little girl had fell in. I shout to a man, "Help, the little girl have fallen in the pond!"
He come over and shout to her, "You is going to be fine!"
She were crying but soon he pulls her out of the water. I ringed for an ambulance and they take her to hospital. She were not hurt.

_____

_____

_____

_____

_____

_____

_____

_____

_____

_____

_____

Year 3

Term 3

Learning Objective: to use awareness of grammar to decipher new and unfamiliar words.

Name: _____   Date: _____

Choosing Suitable Words

When writing good sentences, it is often possible to choose **alternative words and phrases**.
For example - She put on her new hat. She **wore** her new hat.

Task 1   *Add words to these sentences so that they make sense.*

1. She _____ a new dress for the party.

2. The _____ man had grey hair.

3. The _____ crept into the house and stole the _____.

4. The _____ child broke the vase.

5. My _____ baked a cake.

6. He gave his _____ a present.

7. The shopping _____ fifty pounds.

8. The pond was filled with _____.

Task 2   *Re-write this, **changing the word underlined for another**, so that the story still makes sense.*

I <u>looked</u> out of the <u>window</u> and saw <u>an object</u> down by the pond. It was a toy <u>motorbike</u>. I <u>wondered</u> who had left it there. Then I <u>noticed</u> the <u>little girl</u> next door, peering over the <u>fence</u>.
"Could I have the <u>motorbike</u> please?" she <u>asked</u>.
"Yes," I shouted, "I will <u>get</u> it for you."

_____

_____

_____

_____

_____

_____

_____

Task 3   *Find a sentence in your reading book. Write it here. Then **change two words**, so that the sentence still makes sense.*

_____

_____

Learning Objective: to understand that pronouns stand in the place of nouns.

Name: _____   Date: _____

Pronouns

Pronouns stand in place of nouns. For example – Emma was so sad she cried.

Fill in the chart below saying **to whom each of the pronouns below refers**. *The first one has been done for you.*

Rachel took <u>her</u> friend Sam on holiday with <u>her</u> family. <u>They</u> went by plane. <u>It</u> took off at 9.30am. Rachel's Grandma went with <u>them</u> too.

"<u>We</u> are all going to have a great time!" said Grandma.

"Thank <u>you</u> for taking me," said Sam to Rachel.

"Would <u>you</u> like a sweet?" asked Sam.

"<u>Those</u> look really good," Rachel replied.

"Not as good as <u>these</u>," Sam laughed, pointing at <u>his</u> box of chocolates.

her – Rachel	them -	those -
they -	we -	these -
it -	you -	his -

Task 2 *It is often better to use a pronoun than to use a name twice in a sentence.* Correct these sentences adding a pronoun instead of a name. The first one has been done for you.

1. Sally played with Sally's doll.   Sally played with her doll.

2. The cat chased the cat's toy mouse.   _____

3. Mary and Tom visited Mary and Tom's Gran. _____

4. Ella and Ben played at Ella's house.   _____

5. Susie said, "Fiona can have Susie's pen." _____

6. Billy came first in Billy's race.   _____

7. The hamster ran on the hamster's wheel. _____

8. "Would Beth give Beth's book to Dan?"
_____

Task 3 Now look in your reading book and **find a sentence with pronouns in it.** Copy it into your book and **put a ring** around the **pronouns**.

Name: _____   Date: _____

Possessive Pronouns

A possessive pronoun tells us who something belongs to.
For example – The cat is mine. **Other possessive pronouns are my,**
your, yours, his, hers, its, our, ours, their, theirs.

Task 1   *In each of the sentences below, **replace the phrase in italics*
***with a verb and a possessive pronoun.** The first one has been done for you.*

1. The jewels *belonged to her.*   The jewels were hers. _____

2. This pencil *belongs to you.* _____

3. These sweets *belong to us.* _____

4. That bag *belongs to him.* _____

5. This car *belongs to them.* _____

6. That ball *belongs to me.* _____

7. Two of the toys *belonged to him.* _____

8. One of the rings *belongs to her.* _____

Task 2   *Read the following sentences carefully. **The possessive pronouns in these***
***sentences are incorrect.** Correct each sentence and rewrite it on the line.*

1. The cat washed your whiskers. _____

2. My Mum lost their purse. _____

3. "Is this yours bike?" asked John. _____

4. The girl knew the book was its. _____

5. The teacher had their bag stolen. _____

6. The girl went on their holiday. _____

7. The hamster ate hers food. _____

8. The watch lay in his case. _____

Task 3

*Use your reading book to find **six** examples of **possessive pronouns**. Write them on the lines below.*

_____   _____   _____

_____   _____   _____

Name: _____   Date: _____

Using 1st Person Pronouns

The **1st Person Pronoun** is "I" and is used when we write **about ourselves**.
I is used when we write in a **diary**.

Task 1   *Sara has written her diary for the 29th September, the day before she moves house. Read it carefully, then on the lines below* **write the diary entry which might have been written on the 1st October, the day after she moved***. Remember to pretend you are Sara.* **Write in the 1st Person.**

29th September

I am getting ready to move to London. I have packed all my books and toys in my boxes. My dog, Bruno, has gone to stay with my Grandma till we have moved. I will miss my best friend Chelsea and my class teacher Miss Brown. I hope Chelsea will come to stay with me in the Christmas holidays.

1st October

_____

_____

_____

_____

_____

_____

_____

_____

Task 2   *Write the diary entry Sara makes for 29th December when Chelsea comes to stay during the holidays.*

_____

_____

_____

_____

_____

Name: _____   Date: _____

Using 2nd Person Pronouns

The **2nd Person Pronoun** is 'You' and is used when writing
instructions or giving directions.

Beech Drive   Green Road

Task 1   *Read the set of instructions below which
tells you how to get to the local shops. Then, on the lines,
write a set of instructions telling how to get from your house to school*.

1. To get to the shops you need to go out of the house on to Beech Drive.
2. You then walk to the top of Beech Drive to the post box.
3. Then you cross over the road and take the next right, Green Road.
4. You follow this road right to the end.
5. Next you turn left, where you will find the shops on your right hand side.
6. Carefully cross the road and you are there.

From My House to School

_____

_____

_____

_____

_____

_____

_____

_____

Task 2   *Now write some instructions to get from **your table to the playground**.*

_____

_____

_____

_____

_____

_____

_____

Name: _____   Date: _____

Using 3rd Person Pronouns

The **3rd Person Pronouns** are: **he, she, it** and **they.** Those are used when writing **recounts.**

Task 1   *Read the recount written below about 'A Sad Day'. Then write one on the lines below about 'A Happy Day', when Tom gets a new puppy.*

A Sad Day

One day Tom got out of bed and went downstairs for breakfast. Tom's dog, Bobby, wagged its tail and jumped up on Tom. While Tom ate his toast, Mum put Bobby in the garden. She did not know that someone had left the gate open. Bobby wandered out onto the road and was hit by a car. They heard the squeal of brakes and went out to see what it was. Bobby was lying dead in the road. It was the saddest day of Tom's life.

'A Happy Day!'

_____

_____

_____

_____

_____

_____

_____

Task 2   *Now write about a happy day **your friend** has enjoyed.*

_____

_____

_____

_____

_____

_____

_____

Name: _____ Date: _____

Agreement

Every sentence has a verb and a subject. This subject can often be a pronoun. It is important to be sure that the **subject and verb agree**. For example – "I am going out" is correct but "I is going out" is incorrect as the subject and verb do not agree.

Task 1   *Choose the verb which matches each subject. Write the correct sentence on the line below. The first one has been done for you.*

1. I am/is having my tea.   I am having my tea. _____

2. He are/is a good dog.   _____

3. We is/are playing in the garden.   _____

4. She are/is singing a song.   _____

5. They has/have a blue car.   _____

6. You has/have two sisters.   _____

7. We was/were ill.   _____

8. I go/goes to the shop.   _____

Task 2   *Here you have been given the verb in the sentence. Make each sentence make sense by adding a subject. The first one has been done for you.*

1. <u>Miss Smith</u> is a wonderful teacher.

2. _____ were growing in the woods.

3. Katie's _____ lay in the grass.

4. A _____ stood at the end of the road.

5. The _____ was buried deep in the ground.

6. Red _____ were all over the T-shirt.

7. In the _____ lived a giant.

8. Around the _____ came a speeding car.

Task 3   *Copy a sentence from your reading book. Write it into your book. Change the verb in it, so that the sentence does not agree. Ask your friend what is wrong with it.*

Name: _____   Date: _____

Agreement

Every sentence has a verb and a subject. This subject can often be a pronoun. It is important to be sure that the **subject and verb agree.** For example – 'I am going out' is correct but 'I is going out' is incorrect, as the subject and verb do not agree.

Task 1   *Read the following story carefully. **Put a ring around the verbs, which do not agree**. Write the story out correctly on the lines below.*

Last week we was going on a visit to the zoo. It were a sunny day and I were very happy not to be in school. Sally and I had took a big bag of sweets for the journey. When we has arrived at the zoo we was sent to look at the monkeys which was climbing on some tall trees. Suddenly I have my sweets grabbed by one of the monkeys who run to the top of the tree. "I has told you to put them away, Jenny!" my teacher were shouting.

_____

_____

_____

_____

_____

_____

_____

_____

_____

_____

_____

Task 2   *Write another short paragraph about another event at the zoo. **Try to make your subject and verb disagree**, then let **a friend correct it**.*

_____

_____

_____

_____

_____

_____

_____

Learning objective: to be able to use speech marks in writing.

Name: _____ Date: _____

Speech Marks

Speech marks are used in writing to show **the words which are spoken**. The words spoken go inside the speech marks. **The first word** inside the speech marks begins with a **capital letter** and the punctuation mark at the end of the speech goes **inside** the speech marks.
For example – "Come to my house for tea," said Sam. "Thank you," replied Tom.

Task 1 *Put the **speech marks** around the **words actually spoken**.*

1. Please do your reading, Mum said.

2. Can I have a drink? asked Gopal.

3. Sam asked, Will you play with me?

4. Go to bed! shouted Dad.

5. Susan said, I like fruit.

6. Tom said, We had fun.

Task 2 *Re-write the sentences on the line below, **putting in the speech marks and punctuation**.*

1. I am going to the shops Henry said

_____

2. We are going on holiday said Susie

_____

3. Could you do the washing up asked Ben

_____

4. Robert said I had pizza for tea

_____

5. They asked Could you help us

_____

6. Sally said Go away

_____

Task 3 *Copy **two lines of speech** from your reading book.*

_____

_____

58

Name: _____   Date: _____

Speech Marks

Speech marks are used in writing to show **the words which are spoken**. The words spoken go inside the speech marks. **The first word** inside the speech marks begins with a **capital letter** and the punctuation mark at the end of the speech goes **inside** the speech marks.

Task 1   *Re-write these jokes on the lines below adding in speech marks and punctuation.*

Doctor, doctor, I think I'm a spoon said Bob
The Doctor replied Sit there and don't stir

_____

_____

Why did Emma take a pencil to bed asked Tom
To draw the curtains replied Pat

_____

_____

What do you give a sick lemon asked Jill
Lemonade replied Billy

_____

_____

Who's that at the door asked Mr Carr
A man with a drum replied Mrs Carr
Tell him to beat it said Mr Carr

_____

_____

_____

Task 2   *Write a knock knock joke here.* **Remember to include some speech marks.**

_____

_____

_____

Learning Objective: to understand that sentences can be joined using different conjunctions.

Name: _____ Date: _____

Conjunctions

A conjunction is a **joining word**. **A conjunction is used to join two short sentences together**. For example - He went to bed. He fell asleep. He went to bed **and** fell asleep. **And** is a conjunction.

Task 1   *Join these **short sentences** into a **longer one** using **and** or **but**.*

1. The sun came out. The birds sang.

_____

2. Robins can fly. Penguins cannot fly.

_____

3. The story is funny. The story is true.

_____

4. I like apples. I like grapes.

_____

5. An oak tree loses it leaves. A holly tree does not.

_____

6. My dog is large. It is very hairy.

_____

Task 2   *Complete these sentences so they **make sense**.*

1. I like pasta but I don't _____

2. She gave her friend a watch and _____

3. Daniel went to the zoo and _____

4. Nicola wanted to play cards but _____

5. In the tree they saw a thrush and _____

Task 3   *Find a sentence with **and** and another with **but** in your reading book. Write them here*

_____

_____

_____

Name: _____ Date: _____

Conjunctions

A **conjunction** is a **joining word**. **A conjunction is used to join two short sentences together**. For example- He went to bed. He fell asleep.
He went to bed **and** fell asleep. **And** is the conjunction here.
Other conjunctions are **if, so, while, though, since** and **when**.

Task 1

*Join the correct **beginning** to its **ending** and copy it onto the line below.*

Sentence beginnings	Sentence endings
Sam can go to cubs if	so he went to the doctor.
Mr Smith was feeling ill	fell and broke her leg.
While playing tennis Mary	he has finished his homework.
Sanjit finished the race	Tom has bought a car.
Since he learnt to drive	even though he was last.

1. Sam can go to cubs if he has finished his homework. _____

2. _____

3. _____

4. _____

5. _____

Task 2

*Join these sentences into **one** with one of these conjunctions.*

so
while
though
because
when

1. Sam was late. His mum did not wake him.

_____

2. Tina did her homework. She ate her cake.

_____

3. You can have a pound. You tidy your room.

_____

4. We were hungry. We made a sandwich.

_____

5. Sally went back to school. She felt ill.

_____

Task 3

*Find **two sentences** with **different conjunctions** in them. Write them in your book.*

Learning Objective: to understand that certain words can signal time sequences.

Name: _____   Date: _____

Words Which Tell us About the Passing of Time

When we are writing we use words which tell us **about the passing of time**.
These words also tell us about the **order in which things should be done**.
For example – **First**, fill the kettle with water. **While** the kettle is boiling
put a tea bag in the cup.

Task 1   *Read the instructions on how to make a piece of toast. They are in a muddle. **Write them below in the correct order**.*

Now butter it carefully with a knife.

First, take a slice of bread and put it in the toaster.

Finally, eat it!

When the toast has popped up, put it on a plate.

While the bread is toasting, take the butter out of the fridge.

1. _____

2. _____

3. _____

4. _____

5. _____

Task 2   *Finally, **write a set of instructions**, which tell you how to **make a cup of tea**.*

_____

_____

_____

_____

_____

Name: _____ Date: _____

Words Which Tell us About the Passing of Time

When we are writing we use words which tell us **about the passing of time**. These words also tell us about the **order in which things should be done**.

For example – **First**, fill the kettle with water. **While** the kettle is boiling put a tea bag in the cup.

Task 1 *Here are some time words with a letter missing. Complete them.*

fi___st   l___st   d___ring   fina___ly

si___ce   o___ce   th___n   n___xt

w___ile   be___ore   aft___r___ards

mea___while   l___ter   u___til   sec___ndly

Task 2 *Here are some instructions on **how to plant seeds**.*
*Complete them using some of the **words in the list above**.*

1. _____ take a packet of seeds and a plant pot.

2. _____ put some soil in the pot.

3. _____ make a hole in the soil and pop a seed into it.

4. _____ cover the seed with soil.

5. _____ sprinkle the soil with water.

6. _____ wait for the seed to grow!

Task 3 *Write some **instructions** telling how to make a sandwich **beginning each**
sentence with one of the time words in the list.*

_____

_____

_____

_____

_____

_____

Learning Objective: to become aware of the use of commas in marking grammatical boundaries in sentences.

Name: _____ Date: _____

Commas

Sometimes when **sentences are long, commas are used to show where extra information has been given to the reader**. For example – Miss Smith, my piano teacher, is a lovely singer.

Task 1   *Think of some extra information to slot into these sentences.*

1. My neighbour's dog, _____ , is called Sam.

2. On Saturday, _____ , I visit my Gran.

3. My brother, _____ , likes Pizza for tea.

4. Our cat, _____ , sleeps on my bed.

5. For my birthday, _____ , I want a new bike.

6. My mum, _____ , likes to go running.

Task 2   *Put **a ring around the extra information** in these sentences. Next, copy out the sentences **using commas to mark out the extra information**. The first one has been done for you.*

1. My Dad (who has curly black hair) likes to play football.

My Dad, who has curly black hair, likes to play football.

2. Our goldfish which has a lovely long tail has a new tank.

_____

3. My bike which is bright red has a flat tyre.

_____

4. At my school St Peter's Primary we have six classes.

_____

5. Emma my best friend can tap dance.

_____

6. The film which lasted two hours was really funny.

_____